Ice Skating
SCHOOL

Written by Naia Bray-Moffatt
Photography by David Handley

Contents

Ice Skating
SCHOOL

LONDON, NEW YORK, MUNICH,
MELBOURNE, AND DELHI

Designer and Photoshoot Director Lisa Lanzarini
Project Editor Lindsay Fernandes
Consultant Peter Weston
Publishing Manager Cynthia O'Neill Collins
Art Director Mark Richards
Category Publisher Alex Kirkham
Production Claire Pearson

First American Edition, 2004

Published in the United States by
DK Publishing, Inc.
375 Hudson Street
New York, New York 10014

04 05 06 07 08 10 9 8 7 6 5 4 3 2 1

A catalog record for this book is available
from the Library of Congress.

ISBN 0-7566-0267-X

Reproduced by Media Development and Printing, Ltd

Printed and bound in Slovakia by Tlaciarne BB

Discover more at
www.dk.com

Introduction

Ice Skating is a mix of dance and gymnastics, grace and balance, falling over and fun! This book takes you on a journey, from your first wobbly beginnings to the day when you can fly through the air and glide like a swan. You can do it if you keep trying!

Getting Ready

Lilly has been going to ice skating school for a few years and she loves it. As soon as she arrives, she goes into the changing room to put on her skating clothes. It is important to wear clothes that are comfortable and allow you to move easily. Then she ties her long hair back to look neat and also to make sure that her hair is kept off her face. Finally, she puts on her skates. Now she is ready!

Warming up

Before Lilly and her friends go into the ice rink, they do some exercises outside to warm up the muscles in their bodies. This marching exercise makes the muscles in their arms and legs supple.

The skates

When you first start skating lessons, it is a good idea to rent skates from your ice rink before buying your own. Lilly now has a pair of her own skates and is very proud of them. The boots are made of leather with sharp steel blades on the bottom. At the toe end of the blade there is a jagged edge called the toe pick.

Always wear skate guards when you're off the ice.

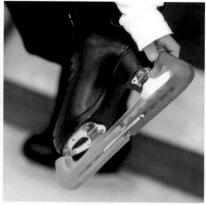

Jamie is in Lilly's skating class. Before he starts to skate, he removes his skate guards. The guards fit onto the blades of your skates. They stop the edges of the blades becoming blunt when you're walking off the ice.

8

Lilly has several skating outfits. They are made of stretchy material so she can move easily, and the long sleeves keep her arms warm. Beginner skaters should wear gloves, too.

A good fit
Skating boots must fit your foot well so that your foot does not move around while you are skating.
It is very important to make sure that your laces are tied securely so that your ankle is well supported.

First Steps on the Ice

Lilly has arrived at the skating school with her friend Beth, who will be taking her first skating lesson. Beth can't wait to learn how to skate! Lilly tells Beth that she will feel a little bit wobbly at first. It's a good idea for her to practise walking in her skates on the rubber floor beside the rink, before she steps onto the slippery ice. Balancing on the blades can be quite tricky at first!

Lilly makes sure that Beth's skates are comfortable and that the laces are correctly tied and tucked in before Beth goes out onto the rink.

Learning to balance

Before you learn how to move on the ice, you need to learn how to stand on it. Keep your head up high and your arms stretched out to the side and slightly in front of your body, with your hands flat to the ice. This will help you to keep your balance.

Joining a class

Beth's teacher is named Peter. He has taught lots of children how to skate. Beth's first lesson will only be fifteen minutes long, but this is enough time for her to learn how to stand on the ice and take a few steps. At first, Beth is going to take lessons on her own. When she feels more confident, she can join a class and learn with others.

Standing correctly

Peter helps Lilly show Beth how to stand correctly on the ice. Lilly stands up tall with her arms stretched out to the sides.

Into position

Peter holds Beth's hand to take her farther out on the rink and get her in the right position for taking her first steps.

Skating together

Beth is still a little bit nervous about skating on her own, so after learning her first steps with Peter, she practices them with Lilly. Holding on to Lilly's hand helps Beth to balance.

Little marching steps

Starting with her feet in a "V" shape, Beth lifts one foot off the ice and places it down again, and slowly moves forward.

Before you take your first steps, you must put your feet in the right position. Bring your heels together and your toes apart so that your feet make a "V" shape.

Lilly has been skating for a few years now but she still falls down a lot. She's used to it! And she's happy to show Beth what to do when it happens.

Letting Go!

Holding on to someone when you first learn to skate may give you confidence. This is important, but sooner or later you have to let go—and the sooner you can learn to skate by yourself, the better. You might not want to let go because you're afraid of falling down, so one of the first lessons you'll learn is how to fall safely and how to get up again. And then letting go doesn't seem hard at all!

Kneel down on the ice

1 Lilly moves onto her knees and puts her hands flat on the ice in front of her. Now she can steady herself before starting to get up.

Falling safely

When you first start learning to skate, you will probably fall down a lot, but even experienced skaters fall, and it's nothing to be afraid of. Since the ice is cold, it helps to wear warm clothes, especially gloves to keep your hands warm and long pants to protect your knees. As soon as you feel yourself starting to fall, try to relax to break the fall.

Lift one leg off the ice

2 Lilly brings one knee up until her skate is flat on the ice and places her hands on it.

Press down with your hands

3 She presses her hands down on her raised knee and slowly brings up the right knee.

The penguin is ready!

It's great to have a friend who can help you skate and give you encouragement

Beth is happy that she has learned to let go.

Sometimes it takes a little encouragement to let go of a teacher's hand. Bending down to pick up this toy penguin, Beth is about to let go of Peter's hand without even noticing she's doing it!

Stand up straight

4   Lilly keeps her head up and slowly straightens both legs until she is standing again.

The end of the lesson
Beth's first lesson is over. It's gone quickly! She says goodbye and thank you to Peter before she skates off the ice with Lilly. Beth can't wait until next time!

Skating Forward

It is now time for Lilly's lesson. She skates in a class with other children, and they have fun learning together. They begin by practicing how to skate forward on two feet, with exercises to help them balance. At first their movements are slow and wobbly, but with practice, they get better.

"Dipping in place"
Bending your knees so that you dip down is a good way to learn how to balance and will help you to skate forward. The students bend down as low as they can before they slowly stand up again.

Dipping in place is lots of fun—once you get the hang of it!

Rosie checks to see if she has bent down as far as the rest of the class. Her friends encourage her to stretch her arms out in front to help her balance, while she dips her body lower.

Off we go

To begin skating forward, the skaters put their feet in a "V" shape and take six little marching steps, lifting one foot off the ice and placing it down again. Then they bring their feet parallel to each other and glide slowly forward.

Ready to skate

Like most of the boys at the ice skating school, Jamie wears a simple long-sleeved top, stretchy pants, and black skates. He can't wait for his lesson to begin.

1 Feet in the "V" position

2 Bend your legs, feet apart

3 Toes in, legs straight

Sculling

Jamie tries sculling which leaves "lemon" shapes on the ice. With his feet in a "V" position, he bends his knees and moves his feet apart. Then he points his toes inward and straightens his legs so his feet move back together.

Gliding

Now that Lilly and her class feel confident skating forward on two feet, it is time to try learning how to glide by skating forward on one foot. You need to be able to do this correctly before you can learn any of the other skating movements. The class starts by raising one foot just a little off the ice and moving forward, before changing feet and gliding on the other foot. The changeover should look smooth and graceful.

Raising your foot

Peter helps Chelleve get used to the feeling of standing on one leg and stretching the other leg behind her.

When you learn to glide smoothly, you will be able to try more difficult things on the ice.

Good balance and poise are very important.

Pushing off

An important part of gliding is pushing off. Start by putting the heels of your feet together at right angles. Then, bending your knees, use your back foot to push your skating foot forward before you slowly raise the back foot. Chelleve leans her body slightly forward and moves the weight onto her skating foot to help her move forward.

Harry feels confident enough to try a dip using only one leg.

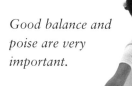

Bending down, Harry lifts one leg and stretches it straight out in front of him.

He then lets go of his foot and tries to keep his arms parallel with his outstretched leg.

" *I feel like I'm flying when I glide on the ice.* **"**

Lilly

Lilly imagines her arms are like the wings of an airplane and keeps her shoulders down to help her balance.

Lilly is a little more cautious about lifting her foot in front of her.

A flowing movement

You really feel you can skate when you can glide on one foot. After a lot of practice, Lilly can raise her foot high off the ice, and by bending her skating knee, she can lift her leg even higher! She stretches her raised leg out behind her and points her toes to help make the glide look elegant and flowing.

Stopping and Skating Backward

*O*nce you have learned to skate forward, you can learn how to stop correctly and how to skate backward. Skating backward may seem quite awkward at first because you can't see where you're going. But when you get used to it, you will find that you can skate faster than when you're skating forward and it's actually easier. Learning to skate backward is a big step *forward*!

James likes practicing the hockey stop. He bends his knees and turns his feet to come to a sudden halt.

Still as statues

The class practices stopping in the "statues" game. Peter stands in the center of the rink while the children wait by the barrier. When he turns his back, the children have to reach him before he turns around and sees them moving. When Peter turns, they must stop by pushing their heels apart and pointing their toes in. This is called the "snowplow stop" and it's the easiest way of stopping. Those caught moving must start over.

Skating backward

Just like when they were learning to skate forward, the class begins with six little marching steps, but this time keeping their toes together and heels apart to make them go backward. The glide between marching steps becomes longer each time they practice.

Backward sculling

Sculling backward helps Lilly to skate more smoothly. It's like sculling forward but in reverse. Lilly bends her knees and pushes her feet apart and then turns her skates inward to bring her heels back together again. She begins quite slowly but gradually picks up speed as she gains more confidence.

Look behind you

Before you start to skate backward, look behind you to see if the path is clear. Once you know there is no one to bump into, you can set off! Try not to look back too often. Keep your head up and arms held out to the sides to help you balance.

To skate backward, put your toes together and keep your heels apart—the exact opposite of the position for skating forward.

The Crossover and Turning

In this lesson, the children will be learning how to do a "crossover," which means that they will be able to skate in a circle. Peter begins by teaching the class how to do a forward crossover, but the crossover can be done backward, too. Then he teaches them how to switch from skating forward to skating backward.

Crossed feet
The children practice the crossover while standing still. They lift one foot off the ice and place it over the other and stand with their feet in a crossed position.

1 Chelleve starts skating forward with her left leg raised behind her and her left arm stretched in front.

2 As slowly and smoothly as she can, she raises her left knee and foot and places them in front. She leans slightly into the circle.

3 Chelleve passes her left foot over her right foot, places it on the ice, and leans slightly inward to make the circle.

Going in circles

Skate blades have two edges that enable you to skate in curves and circles. You will use them all the time in skating. The inside edge is the one facing the inside of your foot and the outside edge is on the outside of your foot.

Chelleve concentrates on her edges when she is skating the crossover. As she crosses her foot, she moves from the outside edge to the inside edge.

"*I love the feeling of gliding before going into a turn.*"

Chelleve

Turning

There are several different ways of turning from skating in one direction to the other. Peter is helping Lilly do a turn called the "three turn" in which you turn on one foot. He takes her hands and moves them around toward him so that she turns her head, shoulders, and body, and then her feet follow.

Spinning Around!

Daniella is one of the older children in the ice skating school, and is a pairs skating champion. Today she is helping Lilly learn to spin on the ice. It takes a lot of practice to be able to spin as fast and as beautifully as Daniella. At first, Lilly will spin on two feet. As she gains confidence, she can start to spin faster, and then later on one foot.

The catch-foot spin

The "catch-foot" spin

There are lots of different spins. Daniella shows the class one of the more difficult spins they can try after a lot of practice. She must concentrate hard on balancing as she holds her free leg up in the air while spinning on the other.

Daniella spins Lilly slowly around, first in one direction and then the other.

Daniella makes sure she is holding Lilly's hands firmly.

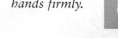

That dizzy feeling

When you first learn to spin, you may feel dizzy. To help Lilly get used to the feeling, Daniella plays a spinning game with her. She holds both of Lilly's hands and turns her around faster and faster.

1 Start by holding each other's hands

2 As you gain speed, let go of one hand only

By bringing his arms close in to his chest, Harry discovers that he can spin even faster.

The "sit spin"

This is one of the spins you will learn. You begin by spinning upright, bringing one leg around in front of you. Then you slowly bend the other knee to lower yourself into a sitting position.

Remember to keep your head up while you are spinning.

❝ I found spinning pretty hard at first, but now I love it! ❞

Daniella

Lilly tries doing a sit spin. Daniella made it look easy, but Lilly finds it quite hard to keep her balance in the sitting position.

Drags and Spirals

Daniella stays with Lilly to help her learn some more skating skills. Both the drag and the spiral are elegant movements on ice that require control and poise. Daniella uses them in competition because they show how well she can balance. With both, you must think about pointing your fingers and toes and creating long, flowing lines with your body. Lilly tries the drag first because it is easier than the spiral.

Lilly looks up to Daniella and loves to learn from her!

1 Begin by bending your knees

2 Then stretch your free leg behind you

3 Go lower and hold the position

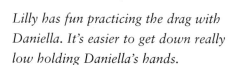

Lilly has fun practicing the drag with Daniella. It's easier to get down really low holding Daniella's hands.

The drag

This is a slow, graceful forward skating movement. Bend your skating knee as far down as you can, while your free leg is stretched out behind you. Turn out your foot so that the side of your boot drags along the ice—but don't let the blade drag, because this will make you stop!

Keep your head up and your leg parallel to the ice.

On a curve

You can skate a spiral in a straight line or in a curve. It is easier to skate it in a straight line, so this is what you will learn first. To skate it in a curve, you need to use the edges of your skate.

The spiral

It's not easy to do the spiral at first. It's hard to keep your knee straight and to keep your raised leg parallel to the ice.

"I am learning to do new things every day and I love it!"

Lilly

To keep her balance as she bends down low for the drag, Lilly must open out her arms.

The supported spiral

The supported spiral must only be attempted under supervision from the coach.

Two's company

Daniella skates slightly behind Lilly so that she can hold Lilly in exactly the right position to support her in the spiral. Peter watches them closely because it is important that they don't get in each other's way, since this would be dangerous.

A Hop and a Jump

In this lesson the children are learning how to jump on the ice. Jumping in the air and landing perfectly on the ice takes a lot of practice! There are many different kinds of jumps to learn, from simple little hops to complicated spinning jumps where you turn in the air before landing. Even the most basic jump should look controlled and graceful.

Lilly practices a basic jump on her own. She concentrates really hard. The more you practice, the easier the jumps become.

The "bunny hop"

Gather some speed...

...and do little jumps, one after the other!

Get ready to land and keep on skating.

The bunny hop

Although it is called a hop, this is in fact a little jump, and it is the first one you can learn. You take off on one foot and land on the other, keeping your arms stretched out.

"Bunny hops
are fun!"

James

The toe loop

The jump below is called a toe loop. You begin by skating backward and take off from a backward edge. As you take off, you place the toe pick of the opposite foot into the ice to give you extra height and rotation in the air before landing.

Holding hands, Lilly and James have to time their jump so that they take off and land together.

Lilly practices the toe loop. She takes off, rotates, and lands without falling. Well done, Lilly!

Jumping for Joy

It's so much fun being able to jump on the ice! Being really good at jumping combines many skills, and you need to be good at skating and have lots of spring. The students are able to do quite a few jumps now, but they are really excited that Perry, one of the older boys at the school, has come to help them practice and to show the some more difficult jumps.

Harry and James are thrilled that Perry has come to skate with them. They hope that one day they will be able to jump as well as Perry.

To get enough height in your jump, you need to bend your knees as deeply as you can.

Turning in the air

In this loop jump, James has to do a whole turn in the air. He pushes off by bending one knee and rotates once in the air, before landing on the same leg he took off from.

The axel is the most difficult jump to learn. Perry has to take off from his left foot, rotate one and a half times in the air, and then land on his right foot!

The "axel"

Pushing forward onto his left foot, Perry gets ready for takeoff.

He brings his arms in to turn one and a half times in the air.

Perry lands on his right foot and then glides backward.

" Perry really helps us! "

Harry

The boys love jumping. In this tuck jump, they see how high they can get in the air. It looks as though Perry is the winner!

Pairs Skating

Today the children are excited because Perry and Daniella will be performing their skating routine, which is known as a "program." It's time for the class to sit and watch the older skaters demonstrate their skills on the ice as a pair. Pairs skating is very exciting to watch, since it combines thrilling spins, lifts, and turns with beautiful skating. Perry and Daniella have been skating together for several years and make these difficult moves look effortless, but it has taken lots of practice and hard work!

The "death spiral"

It isn't hard to guess how this breathtaking spiral got its name! It looks beautiful, but it is dangerous and needs a high degree of skill. Daniella has just one skate on the ice as she lies back while Perry spins her around him, holding her by only one hand.

Finding the right partner is one of the most important things in pairs skating. Daniella and Perry are perfectly matched and skate beautifully together, with precision and good timing.

"*Because we skate together, we have to trust each other and are good friends.***"**

Daniella

1 *To prepare for this star lift, Perry places one hand around Daniella's waist and holds her hand.*

2 *Daniella places her other hand on Perry's shoulder so that she can push herself up.*

3 *Perry bends his knees to help him lift Daniella above his shoulders.*

4 *Daniella then stretches out her legs and arms to create a star shape.*

Lifts

Lifting someone above your head with only one hand requires great strength even on hard ground. Doing it on the ice also requires precision, balance, and perfect timing. Young skaters should never attempt lifts unless they are supervised by a coach.

5 *They hold hands for a moment before Daniella lets go.*

6 *Perry does weight training off the ice to give him the strength he needs to do one-handed overhead lifts like this one.*

Daniella leans back until her head almost touches the ice.

7 *Perry and Daniella smile broadly at the end of their wonderful demonstration.*

31

The Program

It's nearly the end of classes and the students are putting together a show, so that their family and friends can see all the things they have learned. They will each skate in a program of their own, made up of the things they are best at, as well as skating together in a group. Today the girls are deciding what they want to put in their programs. It's a time for the friends to be creative and have fun skating together.

The first thing the girls have to do is to decide what kind of music they want to skate to. Most programs include some slow music and some fast music.

Choosing the steps

The girls want to include all the things they have learned. They can skate forward and backward, spin and jump, glide and drag. Now all they have to do is put all the elements together and time it to the music.

The girls try out a few ideas and quickly realize that some routines are going to need more thought!

Chelleve is good at drags and practices one while Rosie and Lilly watch.

"I enjoy skating to the music!"

Chelleve

The girls laugh together as they create their program.

Chelleve, Lilly, and Rosie have decided on this pose for the end of their program.

Practice Makes Perfect

Learning how to skate beautifully takes lots of practice and lots of hard work. The top skaters practise for hours every day, sometimes trying the same thing over and over again until it's absolutely perfect. Lilly is practising her programme. She wants to skate her best in her performance and tries to get in as much practice as possible before the day of the show.

Skating well is not just about getting the steps right, it's also about expressing yourself. Lilly looks great at the start of her programme.

The artistic side

Like a dancer, a skater needs to make sure that all their movements look beautiful and flowing. The movements of your hands and arms are as important as the movements of your feet.

Peter helps Lilly steady herself and balance while she improves her body line.

He makes Lilly stretch just a little bit further...

It's a great feeling when things go well and all the hard work pays off!

One of those days

There are some days when however hard you try, things go wrong. Even though Lilly has fallen over lots of times today, she won't give up.

Don't worry about falling over. Even in competition, a fall won't stop you winning.

Playing Games

At the end of each lesson the children usually get to play games and relax! Some of the games are organized by their coach, and the children make some up themselves. Some games are fast and some are slow, but all are fun! And even while they are playing, the children are putting into practice all the lessons they have learned.

The girls begin their playtime with a quiet game. They hold hands and see how far they can glide across the ice on one leg, without stopping.

1 Grab each player's middle finger

2 Now skate around trying to tag them

3 Sorry, James, you've been tagged! Well done, Harry!

This is a great game for practicing picking up speed, turning, and bending while having a lot of fun.

Let's play tag!

James and Harry are playing a game of tag with Perry. They begin by putting their fingers together. As soon as Perry lets go, James and Harry must skate away as fast as they can. If Perry catches one of them, it's their turn to be "it."

The girls make up a game called "dizzy heads." They skate around in a circle, and change direction so they don't get too dizzy!

Chelleve, Lilly, and Rosie stand with their feet in the correct position—even though they're just playing a game. It comes naturally to them now!

The "dizzy heads" game

All together now

This game teaches the children that if one skater falls, the rest come tumbling after—just like dominoes. Bending their knees to fall safely, the children lean back and it's slide time.

Show Time!

The day of the show has arrived and all the children are excited and looking forward to performing on the ice. They look splendid in their new matching outfits which have been specially made for the show. Their programmes are chosen and rehearsed and they are ready to skate. Let the show begin!

Look at us!

James and Harry get the show off to a spectacular start. They have chosen a dramatic programme full of athletic jumps, turns and sensational spins. It's fast and fun and they really enjoy themselves.

The boys strike a confident pose at the start of their programme.

The wheel thing

The children enjoy skating the wheel and showing how well they can skate backwards. Holding onto each other's arms, Chelleve and Harry skate a backward curve one way and Lilly and James the other to make the wheel go round in a circle.

It's fun skating all together and working as a team.

Shall we dance?
For this part of the show the children have learnt to do a dance called the foxtrot.

The girls wear pretty bows in their hair to match the outfits they are wearing.

> "As soon as I start to skate, I forget that people are watching me."
>
> *Lilly*

Lilly remembers to keep her head up and smile and enjoy the performance.

Going into a spin...

...and skating out of it.

Lilly's Moment

It's Lilly's turn to skate on her own—the moment she has been waiting for. The empty rink seems very big, but it means she has lots of space to move in. Although she's a bit nervous at first, she is looking forward to showing her family and friends what she can do.

Star quality

Lilly glides smoothly across the ice. She skates her program really well—all the practice and hard work has paid off. The audience loves watching her effortless performance, and Lilly enjoys her starring moment.

Inspirations

Skating with Chelleve has helped Lilly in her performance on her own. She remembers how Chelleve always made sure her arms and hands moved gracefully, creating beautiful lines with her body.

Well done everyone!

All the childen have done really well and are proud of themselves. Beth has been chosen to give each of the class a posy of flowers to congratulate them on their performance.

Skating dreams

Lilly loved taking part in the show and feels a little bit sad that it's over. Lilly's dream is to be a champion skater one day. But for now she enjoys skating with her friends at her ice skating school – and looks forward to many more class performances.

Beth

Lilly

James

Chelleve

Rosie

Harry

❝Ice skating is one of the best things I've ever done!❞

Lilly

Index

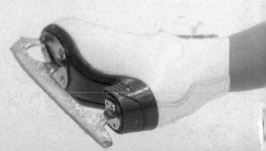

Acknowledgments

Dorling Kindersley would like to thank the following for their help in the preparation and production of this book:

Lee Valley Ice Centre and the School of Figure Skating, Lea Bridge Road, Leyton E10 7QL, UK (www.leevalleypark.com), for their kind permission to photograph the book there.

Special thanks to Peter Weston (BITA Master Coach, Alexandra Palace Ice Rink) for acting as Consultant; students Lilly, Harry, Lillibet, James, Chelleve and Rosie, who were absolutely fabulous at the photoshoot; Perry Drake and Daniella Finch for their participation; Julia March for proof-reading assistance; thanks also to the parents of all the students, for their time, help and patience at the photoshoot.